YOU CAN INTERPRET YOUR DREAMS!

A Prophetic Pocket Guide of Proven Spiritual Strategies
To Accurately Help You Understand Your Dreams

Dwann Holmes Rollinson

Copyright © 2015 by **Dwann Holmes Rollinson**

Sermon To Book
www.sermontobook.com

You CAN Interpret Your Dreams / Dwann Holmes Rollinson

ISBN-13: 9780692378823
ISBN-10: 0692378820

You CAN Interpret Your Dreams! is dedicated to all the
prophetic dreamers who recognize the spiritual language of
love and revelation that can only come from above!
Dream on!

Dwain
Roller

CONTENTS

The Mandate God Has Given Me

Anytime I talk to dreamers, people who dream vivid filmstrip-like dreams, they are quite amazed when I tell them that everyone doesn't dream dreams like they do.

As a matter of fact it's that amazement within these conversations regarding their dream life that seems to usher them into revelatory confirmation that indeed there is something unique about who they are and what they dream.

Most times the amazement doesn't stop there. It just continues to bring about questions like:

- Could all my dreams really mean something?

- Why do I keep having this one particular dream over and over and over again?

- Are you sure I'm not crazy?

- Why do I have so many dreams in one night?

- Does seeing a dog in my dream really represent something evil?

Month after month for years I would answer questions like these so much that I finally decided it would be easier and a great benefit to others to compile the most popular questions and create a simple guidebook on how to spiritually and biblically interpret prophetic dreams.

Though dreams can be very mysterious and hard to figure out, what I have learned after more than 20 years of documenting my dreams is that, yep—when you're a prophetic dreamer—most of your dreams really do mean something.

What I wanted prophetic dreamers like you to know is this: with the right help, **You CAN Interpret Your Dreams!**

And with the right help, you can interpret other peoples' dreams as well.

Though dreams can be very mysterious and hard to figure out, what I have learned after more than 20 years of documenting my dreams is that, yep—when you're a prophetic dreamer—most of your dreams really do mean something.

I've also learned that they don't always mean what you think they mean!

Fortunately, I can actually chuckle at that statement now, because if I knew then what I know now, I would have paid more attention to and even acted upon or moved on what I was shown in my dreams.

After all, dreams are another mode of communication that the one I call Abba Father uses to speak directly to you and me! Once you master the art of learning the language of love He speaks to you and others in, dream interpretation becomes more and more natural.

Discover how natural and easy it can be as I take you on a quick and painless literary spiritual journey inside the pages of You CAN Interpret Your Dreams!

Enjoy!

Meet Dwann

I love educating people on the prophetic because it's the mandate God has given me. So, whenever I get the opportunity, I do my best to educate, enlighten and empower people on the different elements of the prophetic.

Now more than ever, I believe it's important for God's mouthpieces to take their rightful place in the Kingdom and to make sure there is a pure prophetic Kingdom word released when they open their mouths.

Now more than ever, I believe it's important for God's mouthpieces to take their rightful place in the Kingdom and to make sure there is a pure prophetic Kingdom word released when they open their mouths.

I am known as a media expert, a trainer, an author and a prophetic mentor. Years ago, I was a broadcast journalist and I anchored and reported news from TV stations across the country, including Nashville, Birmingham, Alabama, and Savannah, Georgia.

I grew up in Omaha, Nebraska, and reported there as well as in Lincoln. Then, in the midst of a successful TV news career, God suddenly began to speak to me about ministry and He revealed that there was much more He had for me.

He showed me that the platform He'd given me in TV news was just a way to leverage what He would have me do for Him. So I started a small TV production company to help ministries increase their excellence in media.

If you are reading this book, you probably already know that there is much perversion in the prophetic. However, I see God switching that around and releasing pure prophets into the regions.

God released uncommon favor on the company and that is why so many people know me as a media expert.

As a matter of fact, a lot of folks know me more as a media expert than as a prophet, pastor, apostle or minister of the gospel.

But that is changing and God is transitioning me as He allows me to raise up prophets and also exist as a liaison between apostles and prophets, particularly those in the church and marketplace. I'm teaching them how to walk in purity in the prophetic.

If you are reading this book, you probably already know that there is much perversion in the prophetic. However, I see God switching that around and releasing pure prophets into the regions.

One of the ways He has assigned me to eradicate the perversion in the prophetic is by creating prophetic guides like this one, which is Part 2 in my Prophetic Truth series.

The Global Institute Of Marketplace Prophets exists as an international professional company of prophets charged with educating and empowering those chosen to a prophetic ministry.

The mission of GICMP is to provide support, prophetic counseling and education to all Christian prophets around the world who are called to the church or the marketplace.

That's what we do all across the globe. We minister prophetically to different people when they are in need. We also offer prophetic counseling, business counseling, and church consulting for prophets. You can find more about us by going to globalpropheticinstitute.com and prophetdwann.com.

Prophetic Dream Interpretation 101

In the following pages, you are going to learn how to:

1. Awaken the dreamer.

2. Identify the dream language in which God speaks to you.

3. Understand whether or not a dream is about your future.

4. Discover the easiest way to determine if it's time to release a dream to a person you dream about.

5. Release a dream/vision as prophetic release or prophecy.

6. Overcome the fear of dreams.

7. Cooperate with God-communications in your dreams to release your destiny.

8. Figure out why the same dream keeps reoccurring.

9. Learn how your prayer life will affect your dream life.

10. Easily interpret your own dreams and visions.

11. Understand why God speaks to his sons and daughters via dreams and visions.

12. How to retrieve a dream that you seemed to have forgotten.

13) Help others unveil the true meaning of their dreams and the number one action you have to consistently take in order to remember all of your dreams and their meanings.

Here are the foundational scriptures I use when I teach prophetic dream interpretation.

Numbers 12:6 says, "When there is a prophet among you, I, the Lord, reveal myself to them in visions, I speak to them in dreams." This shows us that God is saying, *Guess what? I speak to my prophets in visions and dreams. If there is one among you, I am going to speak.*

Daniel 2:28 says, "But there is a God in heaven who reveals mysteries. He has shown King Nebuchadnezzar what will happen in days to come. Your dream and the visions that passed through your mind as you were lying in bed are these."

In the midst of the craziness of life, you need to just stop what you're doing, go lay down and allow God to minister to you. Then He will reveal what needs to be revealed so that you can manifest His glory.

Daniel 7:1-7 says, "In the first year of Belshazzar king of Babylon, Daniel had a dream, and visions passed through his mind as he was lying in bed. He wrote down the substance of his dream. Daniel said: 'In my vision at night I looked, and there before me were the four winds of heaven churning up the great sea. Four great beasts, each different from the others, came up out of the sea.

'The first was like a lion, and it had the wings of an eagle. I watched until its wings were torn off and it was lifted from the ground so that it stood on two feet like a human being, and the mind of a human was given to it.

'And there before me was a second beast, which looked like a bear. It was raised up on one of its sides, and it had three ribs in its mouth between its teeth. It was told, 'Get up and eat your fill of flesh!'

'After that, I looked, and there before me was another beast, one that looked like a leopard. And on its back it had four wings like those of a bird. This beast had four heads, and it was given authority to rule.

'After that, in my vision at night I looked, and there before me was a fourth beast—terrifying and frightening and very powerful. It had large iron teeth; it crushed and devoured its victims and trampled underfoot whatever was left. It was different from all the former beasts, and it had ten horns.'"

Ask God to reveal to you His purpose, plans and destiny for you. Ask Him to reignite the dream language to you.

In showing you that passage, I wanted to highlight the details that come forward when God reveals prophecy through dreams. Clearly, Daniel saw visions in his head as he lay in bed.

Sometimes you need to stop what you're doing and go lay down or sleep because that's one of the ways God restores prophets. In general, we know sleep is good for us, but I am saying in the midst of the craziness of life, you need to just stop what you're doing, go lay down and allow God to minister to you. Then He will reveal what needs to be revealed so that you can manifest His glory.

How to Awaken the Dreamer in You

This is very simple. First, ask God to communicate with you in your dreams. I speak with tons of people who say they used to dream but not anymore, and my response is that God wants you to dream. And their next question is always, "How do I awaken the dreamer in me?"

Here's the simple answer: Just ask. Ask God to reveal to you His purpose, plans and destiny for you. Ask Him to reignite the dream language to you.

> *It is not as complicated as many make it seem. God speaks to you in your own language. Some of us call Him "Daddy"; some of us call Him "Father"; some may even call Him something different, or they may approach Him in a different way because they are not used to it. But regardless, God speaks to you in your own language.*

If you really want to awake the dreamer in you, it's essential to position yourself around prophetic people and prophetic ministries. Once you do that, you'll begin to see an increase in supernatural communications from God.

So again, ask God to awaken the dreamer inside you, and then find a genuine group of prophets to mingle with. What God is doing in the head and what God is doing in the company, He will do in you as you come into contact and connection with them.

> *Sometimes God will give us metaphorical dreams, which are dreams with lots of symbolism. Other times God will give us predictive dreams, which are about our future and destiny.*

It is not as complicated as many make it seem. God speaks to you in your own language. Some of us call Him "Daddy"; some of us call Him "Father"; some may even call Him something different, or they may approach Him in a different way because they are not used to it. But regardless, God speaks to you in your own language.

If you personally don't use big words, God will not speak to you using big words. Don't overcomplicate it. Yes, sometimes God is going to reveal words that you won't understand, but He is not going to cause your head to explode.

The way you identify God's dream language is to first identify how you speak to others. After that, identify how you speak to God. Then you will be able to understand the dream language that God is speaking to you.

Decipher What Kind of Dream You're Having

Sometimes God will give us metaphorical dreams, which are dreams with lots of symbolism. Other times God will give us predictive dreams, which are about our future and destiny.

But how can we determine if God is telling us about our future versus something else? Most of the time when God is showing you something about your future, it is very specific and precise.

I saw it and then I knew that it was probably going to happen. God was warning me about it, or preparing me so that I could walk through it. He was telling me I just needed to prepare with lots of prayer.

Whether your dreams feel real or not, most dreams appear to be as if you are in them, but we shouldn't necessarily use that as an indicator that it's about our futures.

What's the solution? You must look back at what seems to be predicted, and then consider the timetable.

For instance, last year I was dealing with a pastor, and I had a dream where I saw the pastor was a little bit upset with me. Right then, I clearly knew that this dream was going to show me something in my future.

The dream was something very specific and it related to my current situation. I was in relationship with this pastor who I was helping, so that was very predictive. It wasn't metaphorical; it was a specific situation. I saw it and then I knew that it was probably going to happen. God was warning me about it, or preparing me so that I could walk through it. He was telling me I just needed to prepare with lots of prayer.

When to Know if it's Time to Release a Dream to a Person You Dreamed About

Always ask God first. Say, "God, is this a dream you want me to release to this person?" Secondly, though, you have to pay attention to the prophetic indicators on the inside. Prophetic indicators help us know when it's time to release, when it's time to sit tight, and when it's time to pray a little bit more.

> *Before you release a dream to someone, you must know without a shadow of a doubt that you are not walking in emotionalism, and that you are not walking in anxiety. And in order to do that, you must ask God.*

In Jeremiah, it was like fire shot up in his bones. When I dream about a person, one indicator that signals to me that I'm supposed to release it occurs when I feel my dream almost bubbling up inside me.

Before you release a dream to someone, you must know without a shadow of a doubt that you are not walking in emotionalism, and that you are not walking in anxiety. And in order to do that, you must ask God.

Never get too big for God, or be so confident in yourself that you don't feel like you have to ask God or inquire of Him about something He's shown you in a dream.

Never get too big for God, or be so confident in yourself that you don't feel like you have to ask God or inquire of Him about something He's shown you in a dream.

That's how prophets go astray, and that is how we see the wounded prophets who are hurting left and right like never before. So, again, always ask God and pay attention to the prophetic indicators that He has placed inside you.

How to Release a Dream or Vision as Prophetic Release

This is something people ask all the time, and when I do my training, I get lots of people thinking that they are prophesying to someone ... but all they are doing is just telling them a dream.

If you are not an ordained prophet, you have no right to be correcting anybody. If you have an interpretation, you need to take it to a seasoned prophet and ask them what they think and allow them to do what the Bible says.

I'm here to gently tell you, that's not how you prophesy. Just because you saw a dream or a vision doesn't mean it's a prophecy. Let's learn how to release dreams or visions prophetically.

The Basics of Releasing Prophecy

First of all, prophecy exhorts and encourages and comforts. If you are not an ordained prophet, you have no right to be correcting anybody. If you have an interpretation, you need to take it to a seasoned prophet and ask them what they think and allow them to do what the Bible says. Once all that happens, then it's time for you to release your revelation. You need to be biblical about it and you need to speak as God would because prophecy is meant to exhort, encourage and comfort.

The best thing you can do is find a scripture that applies to your dreams, then prophetically declare that specific scripture and connect it to the dream, and then release it as a prophecy.

Nobody wants to hear discouraging words. As a prophet, you don't need to say it unless you are really sure it's from God.

It's important that if you are turning a dream into prophecy, you speak as God. Now, this takes practice. Some people do it; some people don't—and some people say to avoid it altogether. But I say you should do it, because prophetic words have more weight when they come from God.

Are you confident enough in your dreams and visions to speak for God? To say, "I, your God, am giving you a bright future. Yes, I may have allowed you to go through that hard divorce, but you must know that I am working everything out for your good and releasing joy and I am releasing strength upon you because I care for you and I call you my man of valor."

That's an example of how to speak prophecy in a biblical way, and to ensure that you honored the basics of prophecy, which is exhorting and encouraging and comforting.

Nobody wants to hear discouraging words. As a prophet, you don't need to say it unless you are really sure it's from God. Don't try to give a warning to somebody unless you have been ordained and have been confirmed in some sort of way, and your fruit speaks for itself.

How to Overcome Warfare in Dreams

When you experience evil and death in your dreams, the best thing you can do is declare the blood of Jesus in the name of Jesus. You can do that in your mind. You must recognize that when you have serious warfare in dreams, it could be the enemy trying to invade your spirit.

If I see myself working out a lot, God may be calling me to walk in health and wholeness. Take that information as prophetic instruction and implement it.

Now, there are times when God allows warfare. In those instances, you need to take it as an indication of how the enemy is trying to fight against you, and you need to create warfare prayers that defend against the enemy. Take heed and pray because you do not want that to manifest. You don't want the enemy wreaking havoc in your dreams.

So anytime I'm dealing with extreme warfare in my dreams, I have to take the time to see if there is an open door in my personal life that is legally inviting the enemy to enter this part of my life.

If not, I have to understand that witchcraft is real and sometimes demonic warfare creeps into our dreams because there are folks "working magic" against us.

But always remember, Jesus is Lord!

And as you declare and decree that He is Lord in your life and specifically in your dream-life, the devil will have to flee.

Also, anytime you experience warfare, it's important to examine your life to see if specific relationships may be inviting a level of demonic activity that you aren't ready for.

Lastly, understand that God will give us great warnings in dreams and in order to sometimes show us the seriousness of what is about to happen, He allows us to see the chaos, confusion or even the tragedy within our dreams.

More than anything when this happens, it's time to seriously pray without ceasing and believe that God is your banner and that He will give you wisdom in how to handle every situation.

Also remember the Word tells us "Deliverance is the children's bread!"

Deliverance Sessions

It's good to go through some deliverance sessions for when you have to face warfare in your dreams. I mean the kind of deliverance where people lay hands on you and say, "Come out in the name of Jesus." This will help you be protected at the level you need to be.

Does How to Cooperate with God in Order to Release Your Destiny

First and foremost, you have to understand 2 Chronicles 20:20, which says, "Early in the morning they left for the Desert of Tekoa. As they set out, Jehoshaphat stood and said, 'Listen to me, Judah and people of Jerusalem! Have faith in the Lord your God and you will be upheld; have faith in his prophets and you will be successful.'"

Then you have to understand that sometimes your dreams include prophetic instructions, and sometimes in your dreams you are doing things that you haven't done before. So the way that you cooperate with what God is releasing in your dreams is to take it as prophetic instruction and begin to pray and prophesy over that instruction, allowing it to connect with your destiny.

If I see myself working out a lot, God may be calling me to walk in health and wholeness. Take that information as prophetic instruction and implement it. Don't ignore those instructions. Do something that cooperates with what God is communicating to you, so that your dreams can help release your destiny.

If you're wondering why your dreams aren't manifesting, maybe it's because you are not cooperating with what God is releasing to your mind.

Discover Why You Are Having Reoccurring Dreams

There is a reason why God continues to show you something over and over. It could be that you are being disobedient, or it could be that there is something very specific and strategic God wants to make sure you understand without a shadow of a doubt.

So ask God to release revelation. Ask God to explain to you the importance in the double meaning, or the importance in the double release.

> *God isn't going to do all the work. You have to do your part and ask Him to release revelation to you. Say, "God, I am asking for your revelation regarding _____ because I know there is something here."*

God isn't going to do all the work. You have to do your part and ask Him to release revelation to you. Say, "God, I am asking for your revelation regarding _____ because I know there is something here." Then when you ask Him, understand that He may send a prophet or an apostle or even a child to deliver your revelation.

You must understand that when God begins to do things doubly, there is something strategic He's doing and He wants to release it to you.

Does How Your Prayer Life Will Affect Your Dream Life

If you don't have your prayer life together, then your dream interpretations are going to be less accurate. Yes, there are some people to whom God has given the gift of interpretation, and they can tell you revelation regardless of prayer, but then there are others who need a little help.

If your prayer life is jacked up, then I promise your interpretation is going to be jacked up as well. So, if you want to make sure that you are in constant communication with God—whether you're a prophet or just someone who wants God in your life at new levels—pray often.

If your prayer life is jacked up, then I promise your interpretation is going to be jacked up as well. So, if you want to make sure that you are in constant communication with God—whether you're a prophet or just someone who wants God in your life at new levels—pray often.

Prayer is simply communication with God. It's okay to talk to God. I believe one of the reasons many people can't interpret their dreams is because they simply don't talk to God and ask Him for interpretation.

Does How to Easily Interpret Your Dreams and Visions

Pay attention to how you feel when you are in your dreams. Also, pay attention to what specific things mean to you in your dreams. If I love dogs and you hate dogs, then our dreams are going to have two different meanings. That's why you can't have a blanket approach to prophetic dream interpretation. It does not work.

People often ask, "Why does God still speak to us in dreams and visions?" The answer is simple. Because He said He would. And He does. He says He will pour out His spirit upon us in the latter days, and dreams and visions are the key ways He reveals His mysteries to His prophets.

God is going to release to you His meaning in your own dream language, because He knows that you have a special interpretation, so you have to pay attention to how you feel.

For instance, if rain was coming down upon your head in a dream, would you feel refreshed? Or would you be angry that it was messing up your hair or making you cold? Or would you feel frustrated at first, and then suddenly find yourself appreciating the rain? If that's the case, there's symbolism there. God is showing you that

He created everything, even though you may hate it. Maybe He is revealing spiritual rain that He is bringing upon your life so that you can be refreshed.

So ask yourself what you feel on the inside about your dream. For most people, a snake is going to make you jump. Nine times out of ten, if you see snakes in your dreams, it means witchcraft. It means there is a sneaky someone trying to come upon you and sabotage you.

So be on your guard when you listen to the snake in your dream, and ask yourself if there is someone close in your life that is sabotaging you.

Why God Speaks to His Children Via Dreams and Visions

People often ask, "Why does God still speak to us in dreams and visions?" The answer is simple. Because He said He would. And He does. He says He will pour out His spirit upon us in the latter days, and dreams and visions are the key ways He reveals His mysteries to His prophets.

Why? Because that's how God chose for His kingdom to operate. That's why it's biblical.

How to Retrieve a Dream that You Appeared to Have Forgotten

If you have forgotten a dream, you need to ask God to receive it in the spirit. If you *received* a dream in the spirit, you can *retrieve* a dream in the spirit.

Remember, if God gave it you in the spirit, He will allow you to retrieve it in the spirit.

You can sit there all you want, trying to recall your dream, but by that time, you're operating in the flesh. That's when you need to get in the car and go to a quiet place and say, "God, I need you to reveal my forgotten dreams to me. I didn't do what I needed to do. Please, God, reveal it to me."

You have to be still in prayer until God brings your dream back to your remembrance. I encourage you to pray in the spirit. Don't worry. It's not gone forever. Remember, if God gave it you in the spirit, He will allow you to retrieve it in the spirit.

How to Help Others Unveil the True Meaning of Their Dreams

In order to help others unveil the true meaning of their dreams, you must point them back to everything that I just taught you. Point them back to how they felt in their dreams because that will be a natural indicator as to what God is trying to communicate with them.

Write Down Your Dreams in a Dream Journal

In order to consistently remember your dreams, you must write them down. Back when God was awakening the prophet inside of me, He was giving me filmstrips of my dreams, day in and day out. It got to a point where I had to write them down because if I didn't, I would mix them up.

Even Daniel wrote down his dreams. So remember, write down your dreams. Purchase a dream journal and keep it by your bedside. I leave a blank page after I've written down my dream, just in case God wants to reveal something to me about that specific dream later on.

Then when my interpretation comes in, I can fill in the interpretation. It's so important to do that, especially for those of you who are new in the process.

Write Down Every Detail of Your Dream

Write down the date; write down the colors; be very descriptive; write down every detail you can recall. Describe who was driving what, who was sitting where, who said what, and so on. Because all of those seemingly unimportant details mean something when it comes to God revealing a dream to you.

FAQ

What Does It Mean If You See Your Dead Relatives in Your Dream Interacting With You?

It can mean something good, or it can mean something bad. Necromancy is when we talk to dead people. In the natural world, that's not of God; however, one of the scriptures that many people seem to forget (or act like it doesn't exist) is in Hebrews, where it talks about a great cloud of witnesses.

A long time ago, I had a dream about my paternal grandfather, and he was wearing Mason stuff. God began to show me where my family needed some deliverance, and he was there, and we were sitting in a church—but I never spoke to him. I believe God was showing me the sins of the forefather that we needed to deal with in order to be free in our family.

In recent years, one of my aunts passed away and there was a little bit of conflict happening within the family, and I had a dream about her. In the dream, she told me who was supposed to take her place in the matri-archal part of the family. It was very intense and I felt like there was a message I needed to pass along to some of my family members.

Pay close attention. God may be showing you something that's just beyond what you can imagine. Seek mentorship.

So, if you just sit there in your dream, interacting with your deceased relatives for no apparent reason, and you can't find a biblical meaning, then most likely the dream is not of God.

But then again, there are times when dead relatives come into your dreams and God gives you a reflection of something so that you can see what you need to deal with.

What if You are Scared or Nervous in Your Dreams? As a Beginner, How can You be Sure You're Interpreting Correctly?

Pay close attention. God may be showing you something that's just beyond what you can imagine. Seek mentorship. There is an anxiety and nervousness that is bound to be present when you are first starting out. Ask a seasoned prophet for prayers and advice.

> *The number one reason God reveals things to us in dreams is so we can pray ourselves through them.*

God has not given us the spirit of fear, so any time you see fear in your dreams, it means there is something you have to deal with. Could it be fear of accepting your high call in life? Could it be fear of what seems to be manifesting?

There are times when I don't pay attention to my dreams, and low and behold, the thing I dreamed happens in my life, and I think to myself, "Shoot, I did not pay attention and pray." Because the number one reason God reveals things to us in dreams is so we can pray ourselves through them.

We need to be prepared, not scared. We need to walk with the authority that God has given us.

Does it Mean Anything When You See your Natural Parents in Your Dreams?

Again, we are not going to put a blanket approach to this because this can mean several different things. If you see your parents in your dreams, and they are giving you some sort of prophetic or godly instruction, and you are not used to them doing that, it would be an indication that they probably represent God.

Sometimes God will use people that we respect to impart wisdom in our dreams, because He knows we are more apt to pay attention to them.

Pray, prophesy, pay attention, pray about your dreams, prophesy over dreams, prophesy to your dreams, to yourself, and then pay attention to what's happening. It's simple. Always remember: no revelation, no manifestation. If you don't have revelation, you will never receive manifestation.

Sometimes our parents represent themselves; other times they represent those who have authority over us; and still other times they represent God. But it's not a blanket approach.

For instance, if you are in the middle of a church and your parents yell at you from the pulpit, it could be that they represent your pastor, who is trying to treat you like a child, when that's not their place to do.

If your parents are abusive and you see them yelling at you in church, it could be that they represent someone in authority over you in that church that you are allowing to abuse you.

If your dreams make you fearful, you need to plead the blood of Jesus before you go to sleep, especially if you have lots of demonic dreams. Ask God to give you His dreams.

I encourage everyone to read Psalm 91 before they go to sleep and after they get up. Psalm 91 talks about He who dwells in a secret place of God, but it also battles against that spirit of terrorism and trauma that wreaks havoc against the body of Christ in your sleep. Long ago, my daughter said, "I don't want to dream because I just have bad dreams." But I talked it through with her and we prayed about it, and now she's okay. Again, pay attention. There could be a spirit trying to come against you. Be prepared with prayer.

Final Words of Advice

Pray, prophesy, pay attention, pray about your dreams, prophesy over dreams, prophesy to your dreams, to yourself, and then pay attention to what's happening. It's simple. Always remember: no revelation, no manifestation. If you don't have revelation, you will never receive manifestation.

So you need to make sure that you get the revelation of your dreams so that you can walk in manifestation of your dreams. That way, you can see your destiny unfold.

What is God Saying in Your Dreams?

I want to thank you for reading my guidebook. I would love to hear from you on Facebook and Twitter. If you have a dream that you would like me to interpret, send me an email and I will interpret it within two weeks.

God bless you. If you are interested in more prophetic mentorship, visit www.prophetdwann.com or www.globalpropheticinstitute.com.

Activation Of Prophetic Dreams & Interpretation

Lord I thank you for every seed that has been received on this day as this guidebook has been read.

I thank you that every word that has been read has been received on good fertile ground.

Now, Lord I come into agreement with your son/daughter and I activate and release the supernatural ability to interpret dreams.

I thank you God for an increase in discernment and revelation as your son/daughter yields to the language of love you are communicating to him/her with.

I declare and I decree that even the Gift of Interpretation is being activated and stirred up now in Jesus' name.

I declare and decree that no weapon formed against godly, biblical and spiritual dream interpretation shall prosper.

Even now I awaken the dreamer and call forth every dream that has been lying dormant and every vision that has been smothered and hidden. I call forth a release of strategies and a release of solid understanding in the dream life of your believer.

I thank you God that even over the next 30 days your son/daughter will experience an increase in his/her dream life and that you will even speak metaphors and predictions that cannot be denied.

Lord stir up the gifts like never before. Increase dreams! Increase visions! Increase understanding! Increase interpretation! Increase clarity of mind, spirit and soul.

I break every spirit not like you that would try to invade your son's/daughter's dream life and declare and decree that the spirits of terror, murder, nightmare and chaos will not have their way in the dream-life of your children.

I push back the hand of the enemy and every demonic strategic plan that would be sent to cause the dreams and visions of your son/daughter to vanish and not manifest. I prophesy a hedge of protection around your children as they sleep and slumber and I declare and decree that peace is their portion and I prophesy your son/daughter into a safe place in you that cannot be penetrated by perversion.

I plead the blood of Jesus over your child from the top of his head to the soles of his feed and I say that your dream life is productive, positive and not scary or spooky.

I thank you for the ability to war for the dreams and visions that You have seen fit to release and now God I just say let your Kingdom come and your will be done, now in the lives of every believer reading this prophetic dream activation in the name of Jesus, Amen.

Dream Documentation Exercise

Instructions: Now that you have confirmation regarding the practical steps you can implement to interpret your prophetic dreams, let's take it a step further.

I'd like to challenge you to use this guidebook to document every single dream and vision you have for the next 30 days.

Remember, when you document your dreams it's important to be very specific. For example, if I'm in your dream and I'm wearing a white robe, be sure to document that my robe is white. Colors have meaning just as much as the car you're driving or even the hairstyle you're wearing, especially if it's not the same hairstyle you wear all the time.

But again, the most important thing is to make sure you are detailed in your description and, of course, be sure to date it as well.

Sample Entry

December 24, 2014 — Early Morning Vision: Was in back of some sort of church. Bishop A came in, apparently to change clothes. He glances over and sees me and begins to ask me how I'm doing. I say I'm fine and then he asks me about my daughter Angel. I tell him she is fine and we begin to talk about her and his little one. I tell him they are both beautiful.

Then Bishop B comes in and notices us talking and sits down on the sofa.

When I go back out in the congregation area, everyone is still pumped and soaking in HIS presence. I begin to speak to several folks I'm familiar with who I haven't seen for years.

Day 1

_____

_____

_____

_____

_____

_____

_____

_____

_____

_____

_____

_____

_____

_____

_____

_____

_____

_____

_____

_____

_____

_____

_____

_____

_____

_____

_____

_____

Day 2

Day 3

_____

_____

_____

_____

_____

_____

_____

_____

_____

_____

_____

_____

_____

_____

_____

_____

_____

_____

_____

_____

_____

_____

_____

_____

_____

_____

_____

_____

_____

Day 4

Day 5

Day 6

Day 7

_____

_____

_____

_____

_____

_____

_____

_____

_____

_____

_____

_____

_____

_____

_____

_____

_____

_____

_____

_____

_____

_____

_____

_____

_____

_____

_____

_____

Day 8

Day 9

Day 10

_____

_____

_____

_____

_____

_____

_____

_____

_____

_____

_____

_____

_____

_____

_____

_____

_____

_____

_____

_____

_____

_____

_____

_____

_____

Day 11

Day 12

_____

_____

_____

_____

_____

_____

_____

_____

_____

_____

_____

_____

_____

_____

_____

_____

_____

_____

_____

_____

_____

_____

_____

_____

_____

Day 13

Day 14

Day 15

_____

_____

_____

_____

_____

_____

_____

_____

_____

_____

_____

_____

_____

_____

_____

_____

_____

_____

_____

_____

_____

_____

_____

_____

Day 16

_____

_____

_____

_____

_____

_____

_____

_____

_____

_____

_____

_____

_____

_____

_____

_____

_____

_____

_____

_____

_____

_____

_____

Day 17

_____

_____

_____

_____

_____

_____

_____

_____

_____

_____

_____

_____

_____

_____

_____

_____

_____

_____

_____

_____

_____

_____

_____

_____

_____

_____

Day 18

Day 19

_____

_____

_____

_____

_____

_____

_____

_____

_____

_____

_____

_____

_____

_____

_____

_____

_____

_____

_____

_____

_____

_____

_____

_____

_____

_____

_____

Day 20

Day 21

Day 22

Day 23

_____

_____

_____

_____

_____

_____

_____

_____

_____

_____

_____

_____

_____

_____

_____

_____

_____

_____

_____

_____

_____

_____

_____

_____

_____

_____

Day 24

Day 25

_____

_____

_____

_____

_____

_____

_____

_____

_____

_____

_____

_____

_____

_____

_____

_____

_____

_____

_____

_____

_____

_____

_____

_____

_____

_____

_____

Day 26

Day 27

_____

_____

_____

_____

_____

_____

_____

_____

_____

_____

_____

_____

_____

_____

_____

_____

_____

_____

_____

_____

_____

_____

_____

Day 28

Day 29

Day 30

About The Author

Dwann Holmes Rollinson is an award- winning journalist and Emmy-nominated producer, entrepreneur and media analyst with more than 20 years of media experience.

In April 2001, Ebony Magazine named her 1 of 30 future leaders of America aged 30 and under. Whether in the pulpit, conference hall, classroom or multimedia-seminar, Dwann is a powerful global speaker who brings prophetic revelation and kingdom insight to audiences of all ages and demographics, particularly those called to the marketplace and the prophetic.

Dwann also Walks in Miracles with the manifestation of Divine Healing often experienced throughout her meetings. She is also a savvy business leader & executive coach and founder of Global Institute of Church & Marketplace Prophets as well as, the Executive Pastor of The Worship Place in Jacksonville, Florida, where she lives with her husband Bishop Harold and her blended family of 4 daughters.

Known as a Media Mentor to many, Dwann Holmes Rollinson is an award-winning journalist, Emmy-nominated producer & marketing executive called to leverage leaders into new levels of Kingdom Manifestation. Rollinson combines her 20+ year media background with ministerial insight to show God's Apostles, Prophets, Evangelists, Pastors & Teachers how to easily evangelize on and offline.

As FOUNDER of the **GLOBAL INSTITUTE OF CHURCH & MARKETPLACE PROPHETS,** Dwann is a Prophetic Authority to the Nations called to set-order and build systems of accountability for God's Kingdom mouthpieces across the world.

As Executive Pastor of The Worship Place in Jacksonville, Florida, Rollinson stands beside her husband **Bishop Harold Rollinson**. Together they have founded Global Apostolic Prophetic (G.A.P.) Kingdom Builders Whether in the pulpit or auditorium, Apostle Dwann walks in Miracles, Signs & Wonders bringing healing, hope & prophetic revelation to all, particularly those called to Marketplace Ministry & Prophetics. **"America's DEAN of Divine Design"** Apostle Dwann helps Christian divorcees & overwhelmed college students conquer crisis to move from defeat to destiny! (DwannSpeaks.com)

In April 2001, Ebony Magazine named her 1 of 30 future leaders of America aged 30 and under. As a former broadcast journalist, she was accustomed to reporting the story but now she's called to tell her personal story regarding Christians & Divorce. A story that she speaks on from her experience of how her FAITH, has led her through a recent unexpected crisis to a steady place in the midst of the storm, which is detailed in her upcoming book, **"Life Interrupted: 7 Key Strategies To Overcoming Difficult Times."** Now Dwann combines her Pastoral Counseling skills, as well as her skills as a Leadership Trainer to help people of all backgrounds WIN THROUGH CRISIS.

To find out more about Dwann's personal prophetic ministry visit **www.ProphetDwann.com** and Follow Dwann on social media using **@ProphetDwann**

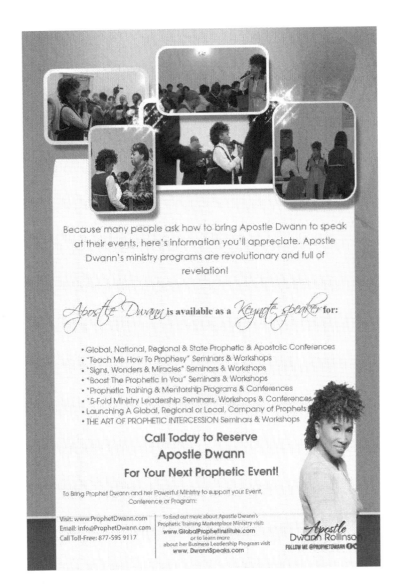

Because many people ask how to bring Apostle Dwann to speak at their events, here's information you'll appreciate. Apostle Dwann's ministry programs are revolutionary and full of revelation!

Apostle Dwann is available as a *Keynote speaker* for:

- Global, National, Regional & State Prophetic & Apostolic Conferences
- "Teach Me How To Prophesy" Seminars & Workshops
- "Signs, Wonders & Miracles" Seminars & Workshops
- "Boost The Prophetic In You" Seminars & Workshops
- "Prophetic Training & Mentorship Programs & Conferences
- "5-Fold Ministry Leadership Seminars, Workshops & Conferences
- Launching A Global, Regional or Local, Company of Prophets
- THE ART OF PROPHETIC INTERCESSION Seminars & Workshops

Call Today to Reserve
Apostle Dwann
For Your Next Prophetic Event!

To Bring Prophet Dwann and her Powerful Ministry to support your Event, Conference or Program:

Visit: www.ProphetDwann.com
Email: info@ProphetDwann.com
Call Toll-Free: 877-595 9117

To find out more about Apostle Dwann's Prophetic Training Marketplace Ministry visit: www.GlobalPropheticInstitute.com or to learn more about her Business Leadership Program visit www.DwannSpeaks.com

Apostle Dwann Rollinson
FOLLOW ME @PROPHETDWANN

About SermonToBook.Com

SermonToBook.com began with a simple belief: that sermons should be touching lives, *not* collecting dust. That's why we turn sermons into high-quality books that are accessible to people all over the globe.

Turning your sermon or sermon series into a book exposes more people to God's Word, better equips you for counseling, accelerates future sermon prep, adds credibility to your ministry, and even helps make ends meet during tight times.

John 21:25 tells us that the world itself couldn't contain the books that would be written about the work of Jesus Christ. Our mission is to try anyway. Because, in Heaven, there will no longer be a need for sermons or books. Our time is now.

If God so leads you, we'd love to work with you on your sermon or sermon series.

Visit www.sermontobook.com to learn more.

Made in the USA
Charleston, SC
18 February 2015